REFECTIONS WITH EMOTIONS

AN ANTHOLOGY OF SHORT STORIES AND POEMS

DR. ALOK DR. MUKTA

Copyright © Dr. Alok Dr. Mukta
All Rights Reserved.

This book has been published with all efforts taken to make the material error-free after the consent of the author. However, the author and the publisher do not assume and hereby disclaim any liability to any party for any loss, damage, or disruption caused by errors or omissions, whether such errors or omissions result from negligence, accident, or any other cause.

While every effort has been made to avoid any mistake or omission, this publication is being sold on the condition and understanding that neither the author nor the publishers or printers would be liable in any manner to any person by reason of any mistake or omission in this publication or for any action taken or omitted to be taken or advice rendered or accepted on the basis of this work. For any defect in printing or binding the publishers will be liable only to replace the defective copy by another copy of this work then available.

Contents

Contents

Foreword

"Reflections with Emotions: An Anthology of Short Stories and Poems" is a wonderful collection of creative writings from various walks of life. The creative writers have crafted their contributions beautifully well. The excellent works of art has been carefully and excellently edited by Dr Alok Chandra and Dr Mukta Goyal. This anthology has come so well balanced work of arts of the contributors ranging from novice to the experienced writers. I am so very excited to go through the rich contributions of this anthology. The various themes of the nature, religion, war, women, empowerment, self-identity, kinship, coexistence, sympathy, love, peace, etc make the short stories and poems very interesting and soulful.

All the creative writings of this enticing anthology are not only informative but also very much enriching and rewarding.

These creative works will certainly help the readers to transform themselves as better human beings with love and care for the self, society and the nature as a whole.

Every story and poem is loaded with a message of emotions, intelligence and wisdom. I firmly believe that these creative works would help the individuals to understand their own self and the universe and the entire humanity.

I sincerely appreciate each and every contributors of this wonderful anthology for their original contributions as well as their commitment for disseminating the real knowledge of the self, various aspects of human relationship, activities of various kinds and the positive side of the society.

My hearty congratulations and best wishes to all the contributors of this anthology. My special thanks and sincere appreciation to the editors especially for their commendable work which has resulted in this beautiful anthology. I wish all the contributors to come up with many more creative writings in the future and enrich the entire humanity with best wisdom ever possible and also make the society as the best version of it ever possible on the planet earth.

This kind of indigenous anthology must be prescribed for the schools, colleges and universities so that in turn so many creative writers would emerge from the society with better work of creative art and this would help the entire humanity to prosper and thrive well in the future with peace, prosperity, happiness and wisdom.

Dr. Saravanan V,

Assistant Professor Senior,

Department of English,

School of Social Sciences and Humanities, (SSL)

Vellore Institute of Technology, (VIT), Vellore – 632014, Tamil Nadu, India.

Preface

The present anthology entitled **"Reflections with Emotions"**: An Anthology of Short Stories and Poems is a garland of meaningful and path- finder collections of short stories and poems.

It is in fact the byproduct of the contributors' innermost emotional intelligence which finds its emphatic as well as real manifestations in the themes of nature, religion, war, women empowerment, self-identity, kinship/coexistence, sympathy, love, peace, etc.

All the creative works of this enchanting anthology are very informative and constructive in terms of knowing the real purpose or goal of human lives.

Moreover, it works as a mentor to bring result-oriented transformation in any society in this cosmic world.

Each story and poem is drenched in human emotions which make the reading public extend their hearty respect and sympathy towards both animate and inanimate objects of nature.

I extend my heartiest gratitude to all the creative writers who have made this anthology an oceanic world of captivating pearls which would in turn prove a milestone in making the readers' hearts and minds packed with humanitarian wisdom in order to witness environmental and social balance/harmony and justice in all parts of the globe.

Dr.Alok Chandra
Dr. Mukta Goyal

List Of Authors

1. When the Father Comes Home…..!

****Vijay Babu**

The sun was about to sink down. The crimson shades of the western skies were getting stained by the blackness of the approaching night. The birds which were late to the nests were hurrying to lull their little ones. The crickets in the bushes were clearing their throats for the nocturnal concert. The smoke of the evening kitchen fires was spreading all around the village.

Little Ambuja was playing with her friends in the front yard of their hut. With her plait swinging on her back, Ambuja was happy.

The big black eyes of Ambuja always stand as a contrast to her patched, coarse little frock on her dark body. Ambuja, the eight-year-old girl is always cheerful.

The small kerosene lamp in the hut was struggling hard to chase the darkness of the hut. Ambuja could be herself during the daytime because it could not have darkness and it would not bring her father home.

'Ammu, where are you? Go and take your bath!', her mother cried.

'Yes Amma'. Ambuja answered her call but did not make any move.

'Move Ammu, your father will come soon, her grandmother, her best friend in the world grunted coaxingly.

The name of her father made Ambuja tremble with fear. She ran in to take bath. She quickly finished her supper and was soon on the stringed cot in the open air. She was not able to sleep. Her grandmother had to lull her with her sweet stories about Princes in magic lands. But she would not turn up now because she was preparing to face her son – Ambuja's father.

The dark night was getting darker. The stars were popping out like lamps on the dark pandal. The village was turning silent. The distant jingling bells of the bullock carts were indicating the arrival of the last bus droppers from the far away from connecting highway. Ammu thought of her father. He would also be becoming.

Ammu liked her father so much just like all other kids. Her childhood was a real story of fun. Ambuja's father was a real nice dad playing, jumping, singing, and telling her stories. He would carry the little Ambuja on his strong shoulders to their farm. Mother and granny would come behind them with their empty baskets for collecting harvest. Father and Ammu would play in the sand and build small castles on the bank of a small stream. While coming back home Ambuja would be with grandma and her parents would carry baskets of maize corn and they reach *home with all love, thrill, and happiness.*

'How nice was father really in those days?' Ambu's reverie broke up with the sudden shouting at the gate.

'Father might have arrived', Ammu felt like running to hug her father's knees. She had a surprise to show to her father today. But the unexpected atmosphere of terror, to which she is getting used to nowadays frightened her.

Ambuja quickly drew her blanket over her face and started listening to the conversation. She could even watch the whole scene through the holes in the blanket. Father came in and slumped himself near the threshold. He was completely drunk and was not even able to stand up. He started talking nonsense.

'They came even today....those idiots' he was mumbling.

'Calm down boy; who came? And why are you trying to make a mess? 'grandma asked.

'Her brothers, Father said showing Ambu's mother.

He was not able to stand and look straight into anybody's face.

'He should have had his glass of that bad drink at the new shop'. *Ambu tried to guess with all her anger against the liquor shop opened recently in their village.*

Ambuja's mother came out to the doorstep from inside the kitchen. The mentioning of her brothers made her both happy and worried. Grandma was making signs to her to go in silently. She was about to make a move.

'Yei, stop there.' Father was trying to stand up and stop her. He caught hold of the door and stood up. The door hinged inwards and he fell straight at his wife's feet. Ambuja suppressed her

laughter but she was aware of the events that would follow his fall. She pitied her mother. She was trembling with fear and when he tried to stand up again, her weak and slender body failed to give support and out of weakness, she swooned down. He stood up and his big black shadow was moving like a demon on the wall.

Grandma ran in and tried vainly to pacify her son. He was like a drunken buffalo with wild horns ready to fight. He pushed his mother down. She started wailing. From his drunken gibberish, Ambu could guess the whole thing. Her father was advised by her uncles not to drink and waste money.

'Yes. Mother says that we don't have our farm now. Since his friendship with Veeru's father, he has changed. Now we don't have even the full square meals. Mother and Grandmother have been working hard to run the family.' *Ambuja felt frustrated.*

'He will never change like Veeru's father.' She thought. Her thoughts flew up to Veeru, the small boy who once studied in her school.

'Veeru has nobody to look after him now except his grandfather. His mother went to jail for killing her husband. She did it out of vexation. What else could she do? She was beaten up every day by her husband. Poor Veeru! He stopped attending school and he is now working as a hawker. He used to hate his father. But my father was not so earlier. He was really nice! Only now…'. Tears of pain were trickling down. Ambuja threw off her blanket and ran out to see Veeru.

When everything came to a standstill and the storm had subdued Ambuja's mother and Grandma came out to sleep outside with a sigh of temporary relief. To their surprise, Ambuja could not be found. They understood the situation. Grand Mother left the house to search for Ambuja. She knew all the places where Ambuja would sit in times of distress and disappointment. She went to the school, to her friend Veeru's house, and finally to the temple on the small hillock. Ammu was there with Veeru.

Veeru the eight-year-old boy was his best friend Ambuja. Grandma felt relieved to see them there.

'Hey Veeru, I have not seen you of late', cheering them up, Grand Ma asked them to move. On their way back home, in the gloomy light of the streetlamps, Grandma consoled Ambuja and asked why she had run out.

'I'm terrified Grand Ma. I felt like seeing Veeru. We both came here to pray to God,' Ambuja explained.

Grandma, who had been praying to the silent God for ages, knew quite well that Ambu had come out to pray to God, out of vexation. She only smiled hiding her disbelief and grief in the age-old wrinkles of her face.

She asked, 'Ammu, what did you pray to God? To punish your father?'

'No, grandma. To change him. To remove that shop from our village. I don't know why they set up such shops?'

'Which shop dear?' grandma asked.

'That bloody shop! All the fathers sit there with glasses …you know? … that shop!' Ambuja continued.

'I love father so much. He was once like the father in my school lesson. Loving and caring for us. But now he comes every night to scold everybody. To beat mother. You and even me. To steal money. To sell away our lands. To grab our food. One day he will even sell me like the villain in the film. I feel like hating him, Granny. Yes. Hate him. See what Veeru's father has done? I hate him. I also hate Valli's father who steals his children's books for liquor. They all beat mothers. They are really bad grandma. They come home only to beat us. Not to live and love us.

Granny, have you ever seen the sparrows in our roof? You know how they love their chirping little ones. Have you ever watched how they spend their time soon after reaching their nests? Have you ever listened to their happy voices? Is my father like that? Does he love us? I really wanted to show you the prize I won in the competition today! Has he got any interest in me? I love my father but he is forcing me to hate him.' Little Ambu started crying and sobbing, sobbing like the broken earth.

Grand Mother was too moved to stop the flow. Unable to drag her old feet and with a heavy heart, she took the child to her bosom. The tears welled up in the forlorn heart of granny broke out like the rain of the old skies. The small doll which Ambuja won in her school as a prize and which Ambuja wanted to show to her father as a surprise remained as a mute witness of pain beside the pillow.

2. Transformation : An Emotional Story of Ignorance and Self-refinement

** *Dr Alok Chandra*

Pranav has recently completed his 10ᵗʰ board exam and is on the way to his school. The name of his school is Vidya Niketan and is 5 KM away from a wild forest.

Pranav has now reached his destination; he sees a row of students standing near the official noticeboard. Eventually he listens to a voice which is not strange to him. Santanu is his fellow batchmate and is the most authentic or befitting example of a real friend. Pranav still has not forgotten the incident which took place near the outskirt of his vilkage. It was the exact time of the fruitation of seasonal mangoes. The watchman was a moody person and never permitted any person to come inside the cultivated area. That is why the local boys made a plan to get up early in the morning and pluck the ripped fruits so that they may relish its delicious or sweet taste. The boys were ignorant and they had no idea about the consequence of their actions. All of them were not even 18-year-old. Pranav was deeply absorbed in stealing the mangoes while Santanu is on the ground keeping his vigilant eyes on the watchman. But it was definitely the fate of that particular day that they were seen and grabbed by the clever guard. Pranav tried his utmost to get himself free from this unwholesome situation but he fell down the surface of the ground. He felt a severe pain in his body; he could not control his anger ; he saw a stone and threw the same on the old watchman as a revenge in order to punish him. Santanu looked at the watchman's face and got frightened to find a pour of blood on his wrinkled forehead. The old man's wet eyes seemed to take the shape of an ocean wherein it was impossible for any person without having supernatural powers to fathom the depth of water.

Pranav accompanied by his friend reached his house. His mother Saroja Devi had already discharged her cooking work by that time. She did also see her son's fast friend. The clock ringed an alarm of 2 o'clock that also indicated the lunch time for the whole family. Pranav out of curiosity asks his mother about his father. Saroja Devi Said, "It is the peak of the summer season. Dhaniram Ji is engaged in the agricultural works but is going to join us soon".

Santanu's mind was totally disturbed due to his friend's hostile action towards an aged person. He secretly advises Pranav to disclose today's incident before both his father and mother; he was worried about the watchman's pathetic condition after seeing his wounded forehead. Meanwhile Dhaniram babu enters into his house. Pranav looks at his father's fatigue face ; he observes layers of sweat on his face which is the proof of his untiring commitment towards his agricultural and domestic duties. Pranav feels guilty of his insensible actions as his father is a pious person and there is always the manifestation of real humanitarian or moral virtues and values in his familial, professional and social works or duties. Honesty is the real hallmark of his personality.

All the persons have finished their today's lunch. Pranav takes the ongoing or present moment as the most suitable opportunity to unhide today's incident before his parents.

Dhaniram babu is an experienced person ; he does not slap on his son; Instead teaches him the lesson of compassion, honesty, hard work, etc.

Santanu feels relaxed after observing Dhaniram babu's sensible behavior towards him and his friend. Saroja Devi plucks satisfactory number of guavas from a tree of her domestic garden. She takes an earthen pot and makes it full with green and sweet guavas; she happily hands over it to Santanu. Pranav has become a transformed youth now. He has gone through consistent self-refinement in his humanly life. He is thankful to his parents and teachers for mending his personal/educational life with noble humanly traits.

The memory of his past life is now interrupted after he receives a bunch of congratulations from his teachers and friends for his emphatic performance in the board exam. Santanu has also done well in all the papers of that particular exam. Both the friends now decide to return to their v

3. A Smart Vendor

****Dr. Joseph Kumar Kukumanu**

It was so rushed that day in Grand Trunk Express from Delhi bound Chennai. The clock is rushing towards noon and the general compartment is hustling with people fighting for seats. However, there were some people who somehow found a piece of place to sit but try not to accommodate anyone next to them. They sit stretched on their seats and bother to neither look at anyone nor even listen to them. Somehow I got a seat in the third station after boarding the train. Everyone has only one game to play; the waiting game of travelling. Being the month of March, the compartment seems to be heating up with the scorching sun in the sky and with the smokers who recklessly choose to light their cigarettes. Somehow after a couple of stations, I could see some got a seat to sit and rest.

With each station passing by 10 new inmates entered the compartment while some 10 got down. However, there are occasional vendors selling peanuts, guavas, and some lady vendors selling jasmines. I always wonder about the life of these vendors. Even if the compartment is bustling with people, they still make their way into the compartment and do their business. In fact, they appreciate more crowds in the compartment to do their sales. Some people who love sleeping occupy the berths meant for luggage in a general compartment and take quick naps while some chit chat in the compartment as if they are in their favourite place enjoying life. I wondered at all these when someone handed me over Rs.10 note and asked to pay for the Palli wala and asked the packet to be passed it on to him. I felt like laughing. Everyone is enjoying the journey except me as that was the tenth time I scolded myself for not booking my ticket prior. But I knew pretty well that I cannot book the ticket as my wife went for delivery and the date of delivery was extended by three days. As a precaution, I did not reserve my ticket to avoid cancellation and reserving the ticket again. Hence my regret was only a little as my heart is bubbling to meet the newborn baby boy in the home town. My heart was overjoyed and was not minding the din of the compartment.

Vendors kept coming and making their sales in the compartment with ease as people in the general compartment usually come prepared with extra change to buy some snacks. I had a quick nap for fifteen minutes and then I was up again and sat properly and waited for Vijayawada station. Then there entered a Samosa vendor into the compartment shouting, 'Samose bees ka teen, bees ka teen'. The aroma of samosas went around the compartment at once. I suppressed my strong desire to buy samosas and eat as the pricing appeared a little high. I peeked into his basket as he passed by to find that samosas were a bit big and delicious. I felt sorry for not buying. In fact people think differently about the pricing. They appear to think about what happened to fifty paise while calculating each samosa at Rs.6.50ps instead of thinking at the one rupee discount that was getting when each samosa calculated at Rs7 per piece. However, the guy in the next row purchased and started eating. Somehow many did not dare to buy at that pricing. By the time, the guy moved to another compartment, there came another samosa vendor shouting 'bees ka chaar, bees ka chaar". Everyone this time felt the pricing to be a little ok and started buying samosas chuckling at the guy who purchased the samosas at bees ka teen. The guy felt rather insulted but bore the brunt in his heart. Everyone started munching samosas loudly. This time, I felt like buying samosas and bought for twenty rupees. I started eating silently.

Meanwhile, by chance, the guy who sold samosas at bees ka teen could not make sales well, came back into the compartment shouting 'bees ka chaar bees ka chaar.' The shouting sounded still more irritating for the guy who purchased them at three for twenty. Meanwhile, others who failed to buy even bees ka chaar but waiting for bees ka paanch this time also bought from the vendor who revisited the compartment and started munching samose delightfully and chuckling at the guy who purchased samose three for twenty.

The situation turned out to be a little more irritating for the guy and he felt like questioning the vendor as to why he cheated him with bees ka teen. I started looking at the situation as to what would happen. The vendor was very smart and said, Sahab, thab ka rate woh thee ab ka rate ghat gaya, ab lelo bees ka chaar" (he said that it was three for twenty last time, now it has been reduced you can buy four for twenty now") The guy could not think twice but bought the samose at four for twenty. This time I felt like laughing as to think that we cannot beat a shopkeeper in his business tact as we hardly see a shopkeeper once in a month while a shopkeeper sees a hundred customers on daily basis. The smart vendor this time had his sales up.

In fact, none of the people in the compartment understood that it was a trap that they were in. Both the samosa vendors planned to sell their stuff in a typical way as usual. The first vendor comes with a higher price tag and fills the minds of the people in the compartment that samose are delicious with a kind of aroma. Then the second vendor comes with the same stuff but with a decent price tag. This time half of the compartment would buy the stuff while the other half wait for the third vendor who would offer them five for twenty. But as planned there would be no third vendor but the same first vendor revisits with discounted pricing. This time, the rest of the people would feel as if they won the deal and buy the stuff. As there would be no one to sell at their expected pricing, people would think that made the best deal ever.

After all samosa business is a high paid job for those who seek to sell in the compartments with one rupee margin being paid on each of the samosa being sold and make as much as a thousand rupees per day on an average.

4. Kathmandu: A place to visit

**** Dr. Deepesh Kr**

The domino metaphor is uniquely appropriate in this story. It's set in Nepal, my second home since 1979, my mothers' birthplace under the ancient state of Mithila, goddess Sita at Janakpur. Nepal is perhaps one of the best countries that I have visited. It has everything, from amazing natural diversity, wildlife, and cultural ethos to the awe-inspiring Himalayas. Nepal is a country of many wonders with treasures that never fail to amaze and inspire me. As much as Nepal, I wanted to really dive deep into the historical and cultural aspects of the country. After all, Nepal has ten UNESCO World Heritage Sites, and despite its growing modernization in places like its capital Kathmandu and other major cities, the tenor of cultural spirit is still alive and thriving in almost all corners of Nepal- sometimes even mingling along with the rapid growth of cities and their rapid in-migration. Speaking of Kathmandu, the capital of Nepal is like any other, always bustling with life and energy and chaotic pandemonium. When I arrived at the Tribhuwan International

Airport in Kathmandu. The first thing I noticed about Nepal was its people. Kind and friendly, ready to help someone in need. This may be a cliché statement you hear from most travelers regarding the country they traveled to. However, I'm saying so because of what I've witnessed between the citizens themselves, rather than how they treated me as a visitor. Little things I have witnessed among the people make me believe that the Nepali people truly are a wonderful bunch. It is shown in the way bus conductors and passengers alike keep the bus waiting for that last passenger who is lagging behind. It is evident in how the motorist smiles and waves of a kid who runs onto the street after his ball. The people are like a hot bowl of soup on a rainy day; always warm and soothing. Conversations strike up as naturally as if you have known each other for years. All the people I met during my trip made me feel at home and made my journey an unforgettable one. Surrounded by the majestic Himalayas on all sides, Nepal certainly abounds in pristine natural beauty. Be it the snow-capped peaks of the Himalayan ranges or the tranquil valleys, most of Nepal looks just like an image turned reality from your childhood fairy-tale book. Apart from that, the country has plenty to offer to the cultural traveler. Being a melting pot of Buddhist and Hindu ideologies, Nepal has a rich history that is unique and enchanting. From massive Hindu temples to quaint Buddhist monasteries and architectural masterpieces, Nepal has it all. The best thing — a large number of Nepal's top-rated cultural and historical attractions are located in and around Kathmandu, the capital city.

First on my tour list was the heritage sites of Kathmandu itself. A bit about Kathmandu before we delve into its cultural and historical treasures; Kathmandu is the largest city of Nepal, with a population of about 1.5 million people. Historically termed as "Nepal Mandala", Kathmandu has been the home of Newari culture since medieval times. The Newari culture is definitely seen in various aspects of the city, from temples, the architectural style of buildings, food, and even celebrations and festivals. The historical sites of Kathmandu manifest the Newa architecture quite beautifully. Moreover, Kathmandu has been, for many years, the epicenter of the Himalayan country. It has a multiethnic population and has many Buddhist and Hindu religious sites, including heritage sites. Kathmandu (/ˌkætmænˈduː/; Nepali: काठमाडौँ, Nepali pronunciation: [ˈkaṭʰmaɳḍu]), officially the Kathmandu Metropolitan City (Nepali: काठमाडौँ महानगरपालिका), is the capital and most populous city of Nepal with 975,453 inhabitants in 2011. It is located in the Kathmandu Valley, a large valley in the high plateaus in central Nepal, at an altitude of 1,400 metres (4,600 feet). The valley was historically called the "Nepal Mandala" and has been the home of the Newar people, a cosmopolitan urban civilization in the Himalayan foothills. The city was the royal capital of the Kingdom of Nepal and hosts palaces, mansions, and gardens of the Nepalese aristocracy. It has been home to the headquarters of the South Asian Association for Regional Cooperation (SAARC) since 1985. Today, it is the seat of government of the Nepalese republic, established in 2008, and is part of the Bagmati Province. Kathmandu is and has been for many years the centre of Nepal's history, art, culture, and economy. It has a multiethnic population within a Hindu and Buddhist majority. Religious and cultural festivities form a major part of the lives of people residing in Kathmandu. Tourism is an important part of the economy in the city. In 2013, Kathmandu was ranked third among the top ten upcoming travel destinations in the world by Trip- Advisor and ranked first in Asia. The city is considered the gateway to the Nepalese Himalayas and is home to several World Heritage Sites: the Durbar Square, Swayambhunath, Boudhanath and Pashupatinath. Kathmandu valley is growing at 4 percent per year according to the World Bank in 2010, making it one of the fastest-growing metropolitan areas in South Asia, and the first region in Nepal to face the unprecedented challenges of rapid urbanization and modernization at a metropolitan scale. The indigenous Nepal Bhasa term for Kathmandu is Yen. The Nepali name Kathmandu comes from Kasthamandap, which stood in the Durbar Square. In Sanskrit, Kāṣṭha (Sanskrit: काष्ठ) means "wood" and Maṇḍapa (Sanskrit: मण्डप) means "pavilion". This public pavilion, also known as Maru Satta in Newari, was rebuilt in 1596 by Biseth in the period of King Laxmi Narsingh Malla. The three-story structure was made entirely of wood and used no iron nails nor supports. According to legends, all the timber used to build the pagoda was obtained from a single tree. The structure collapsed during a major earthquake in April 2015. The colophons of ancient manuscripts, dated as late as the 20th century, refer to Kathmandu as Kāṣṭhamaṇḍap Mahānagar in Nepal Mandala. Mahānagar means "great city". The city is called Kāṣṭhamaṇḍap in a vow that Buddhist priests still recite to this day. Thus, Kathmandu is also known as Kāṣṭhamaṇḍap. During medieval times, the city was sometimes called Kāntipur (Sanskrit: कान्तिपुर). This name is derived from two Sanskrit words – Kānti and Pur. Kānti is a word that stands for "beauty" and is mostly associated with light and Pur means place, thus giving it the meaning, "City of light". Among the indigenous Newar people, Kathmandu is known as Yeṃ Deśa (Newar: यँ देश), and Patan and Bhaktapur are known as Yala Deśa (Newar: यल देश) and Khwopa Deśa (Newar: ख्वप देश) respectively. "Yen" is the shorter form of Yambu (Newar: यम्बु), which originally referred to the northern half of Kathmandu. The older northern settlements were referred to as Yambi while the southern settlement was known as Yangala. The spelling "Katmandu" was often used in older English-language texts. More recently, however, the spelling "Kathmandu" has become more common in English.

Once a collection of warring states, the Kingdom of Nepal came into being as a single state in 1769, when Prithvi Narayan Shah, the Raja of Gorkha, conquered his neighbours and defeated the Malla kings of Kathmandu to form an amalgamated single kingdom. He became Nepal's very first king, and legend has it he forged a poisoned chalice for future generations of rulers, though it's hard to see how he can be blamed. As he approached Kathmandu with his armies he passed a sadhu (or holy man) on the trail who asked him for a bowl of curd. Not one to shirk his religious duties, Prithvi Narayan Shah presented the food, but the sadhu's table manners proved a little rustic. After he finished eating he vomited his meal into a cup and offered it to the Raja to drink. Understandably, Prithvi Narayan Shah wasn't altogether delighted with the sadhu's gratitude; he grabbed the cup out of the sadhu's outstretched hands and threw the contents back at him. This may not have been the politest thing he could have done, but if this was churlish the sadhu's reaction was even more so. He was furious and stood up to curse the Raja in front of his followers. "If only you had swallowed your pride and drunk the curd, I could have granted you every wish," he proudly boasted, doing what many drunk men have done before and since by trying to look dignified while caked in vomit. "Instead I will send you a curse. You will go on to conquer Nepal, but your family will rule for only ten generations. At the end of the tenth generation, the Shah Kings will be no more." While this clearly sounds like beer talk to you and me, amazingly the sadhu's words ended up coming true. On 1 June 2001, Crown Prince Dipendra walked into the Royal Palace in Kathmandu and shot dead his father King Birendra, his mother Queen Aishwarya, his sister Princess Shruti, his brother Prince Nirajan, and five other members of his family, before turning the gun on himself. His uncle Gyanendra was away from Kathmandu at the time and was crowned king, but he reigned *for only seven years before Nepal's volatile political situation moved on. In 2008 Gyanendra was deposed and the monarchy abolished. They had been the 10th generation of Shahs to rule Nepal. Things were less than smooth before that. Prithvi Narayan Shah's son and successor Pratap Singh managed to produce a son by his wife Queen Rajendra Laxmi, but then absent-mindedly took a second wife Maiju Rani who was of the wrong caste (the Hindu equivalent of using the wrong handshake) and made her pregnant. This wasn't ideal for the succession, and it wasn't helped by the king spent much of his time indulging in sexual tantric rites with his second wife under the influence of opium. Luckily Pratap Singh died of smallpox before the second child was born. Queen Rajendra Laxmi allowed her rival to give birth, but then made her perform sati (or burn herself to death). This more or less set the tone for the rest of the Nepalese succession. Pratap Singh's second son, Sher Bahadur Shah, ended up murdering his first one, Rana Bahadur, with a sword during a royal audience many years later, before being strangled to death by a Kazi called Bal Narsingh Konwar (that's a royal bodyguard, rather than a euphemism for a toilet). A descendant of the kazi, Jung Bahadur Konwar, seized power in 1846 following another infamous royal massacre known as the Kot Massacre, which saw 30 members of the Nepalese aristocracy slain. He started up a new dynasty, the Rana Dynasty, which became Nepal's hereditary prime minister. The Ranas were effective rulers of Nepal until 1951, and the Shah royal family lived through this period as little more than a puppet monarchy. As you can see, the history of the Nepalese royal family is a colourful one which rather puts the troubles of the British royal family — who mainly have to worry about the paparazzi taking long-range photographs of them with their tits out — into context. For most of its history, Nepal remained in isolation behind the natural defences of the Himalayas, and its rulers were content to avoid communication with the outside world.*

While the British were exploring the high peaks of the Himalayas throughout their Indian empire — in Kashmir and Baltistan in the west, and Darjeeling and Sikkim in the east — and gaining permission from the Tibetan government to approach Everest from the north, Nepal's borders, containing some of the jewels of the Himalayas, remained firmly closed.

Shree Pashupatinath Temple: - *The Holiest of the shrine*

At the present place where the temple of Pashupatinath rests, there used to be a mound. A cow frequented this mound and offered her milk there. A cowherd noticed this strange occurrence and out of curiosity, dug at this spot. As he began digging a great light poured out. The light had come out from a linga with faces of Shiva carved on four sides. The people built a shrine to shelter this linga. This shrine came to be known as Pashupatinath, dedicated to Lord Shiva in his incarnation as Pashupatinath, the protector of animals. Thus no animal is sacrificed within the temple. Situated 5-km east of Kathmandu, and lying on the banks of the holy river Bagmati, the two-tiered pagoda temple with heavily gilded roofs includes many small temples, dharamshalas, bathing, and burning ghats (where the last rites for the dead are performed). The ornate silver doors of the temple are closed to non-Hindus. But one can clearly see the temple and rituals being performed from the eastern bank of the Bagmati River. The temple is listed in the UNESCO World Heritage Monument List. The temple comes alive during Maha Shivratri, the night of Lord Shiva, which falls in the month of February/March. Thousands of pilgrims flock to the temple to celebrate the night dedicated to Lord Shiva. Another festival that is celebrated at Pashupatinath is Teej. This festival is celebrated in the month of Bhadra (August/ September). On this day women observe a fast and pray to Lord Shiva for the long, healthy and prosperous life of their husbands. From dawn, a long line of women dressed colorfully in red saris and green pote (glass beads), carrying an offering to Lord Shiva can be seen. Many of them dance and sing in groups while waiting for their turn to worship at the shrine.

The city was wrapped in clouds and the pilot had to circle the plane in the air in hope that the clouds will disperse. It wasn't even sure we were going to land in Kathmandu as we received a message we could head to another country if the clouds refuse to move away. Forty minutes later, while we were racing down the concrete airport runway, **I thought to myself: "Nature is king in Nepal"**. And the more I walked around Kathmandu, the more I saw this thought materialize in the city around me. **The whole city is practically nested in the Himalayan Mountain: a guardian that protected Nepal from invasion through the past centuries, but also a mighty force capable of causing destruction.** I spoke with a Nepali friend of mine who told me proudly **"we don't celebrate Independence Day in Nepal, because we were never an occupied country"**. The reverence of people for the surrounding mountains is contagious and stays with me to this day. Walking the streets in Kathmandu, you can notice that, truly, Nature has the last word in Nepal. As such, Kathmandu city hosts four major UNESCO Sites. In the Kathmandu Valley, there are a total of 7 UNESCO World Heritage Sites. The UNESCO Sites are distributed among the valley closely to one another. That makes the Kathmandu valley have one of the densest concentrations of UNESCO World Heritage Sites that are situated alongside each other. Within the city itself, the four major sites are the temple of Pashupatinath, the Swayambhunath Stupa, the Bouddhanath, and the Kathmandu

Durbar Square. My first site was the holy Hindu temple of Pashupatinath. A major sacred Hindu temple, Pashupatinath is located on the banks of the Bagmati River. Inscribed in the UNESCO World Heritage Site list in 1979, Pashupatinath is a large complex with many smaller temples, ashrams, and sculptures. When I visited Pashupatinath, I saw many worshippers, many with bright red tikka on their foreheads. During the major festival of Maha Shivaratri, Pashupatinath Temple was swarmed by many pilgrims from all over the country, with many from India as well. I also saw many Sadhus in the temple, with their faces covered in ashes and donning bright yellow robes with matted hair. I was also informed that the temple is also where the Hindu people performed their sacred cremation ceremony by the banks of the river. The pagoda style of the Pashupatinath temple is something that I was to come across many times during my tour. The beautifully crafted two-level roofs of the temple are balanced on wooden rafters which are decorated with amazing carvings. With the atmosphere rich with burning incense, the temple was quite exotic and reflected the cultural beauty in the constant peal of its temple bells. My next UNESCO Site was the Kathmandu Durbar Square. One of the three Durbar Squares of the Kathmandu valley, the Kathmandu Durbar Square holds the palaces of the old Malla and Shah Kings of the Kathmandu city, along with many temples, old buildings, and monuments along with sculptures and statues of Gods. The place was as busy as ever, with small vendors selling spices and flowers and shops of Thanka paintings and Nepali handicrafts that ranged from brass and copper jewelry to traditional Newari masks and Nepali paper Mache. The complex itself was beautiful. Despite the damage done by the earthquake, it is easy to see the wonderful Nepali craftsmanship on the temples and buildings of Durbar Square. The tentatively ornamented doors and windows of the temples and the finely tuned and crafted sculptures of the various gods seemed lively. It was not hard to imagine how it must have been in medieval times. The openness of the complex and being surrounded by such majestic culture and architectural beauty had me in a trance. The people going about their way, with the looming temples and the giant statue of the God, with flocking pigeons and the bustling atmosphere seemed to breathe life into the area.

After a quick lunch of delicious food of Nepal in one of the many restaurants in the Durbar Square area, I headed out to the Swayambhunath temple- also known as "the Monkey Temple", an ancient religious temple atop a hill west of the city. At the entrance of the temple, I saw three giant statues of Buddha, all decorated quite beautifully, along with gumbas and smaller stupas which were also quite elaborately decorated and painted in the most intricate colors. My guide told me that each morning before dawn, hundreds of Buddhist and Hindu pilgrims ascend the long steps from the eastern side that lead up the hill and begin a series of clockwise circumambulations of the Stupa. After I had climbed the steps up to the Stupa myself, I was rewarded with the most breathtaking sight of the panoramic city, which seemed to be alive. After a tour of the temple complex, my next destination was the Bouddhanath Stupa. As I was in the car being driven to Buddha, I also got a chance to experience the hectic traffic of the city; it truly is quite fascinating! Bouddhanath is the largest Buddhist Stupa in Nepal. When I reached Bouddhanath, the beautiful dome of the Stupa loomed up in front of me like a giant. The sire of the Stupa was decorated with many colorful prayer flags and the serene eyes of the Buddha looking out in four directions were quite majestic in the evening sun. The sparse distribution of the twilight clouds above the Stupa gave off a tranquil feel to the whole place. There were many people around here as well, sitting by on the base of the Stupa and enjoying the evening with family and friends. It was a lovely site to end my first day of the tour. Nepal really is a wonderful country with amazing features and beauty. It simply isn't enough to visit it once, as the country has so many attractions and highlights that it demands more well-deserving visits. It's natural, Himalayan, cultural, and religious wonders make Nepal a cornucopia of exotic characters.

I read a stack of magazines and books about Mount Everest in closet, including the 1953 issue of National Geographic featuring a cover story about the first-ever successful ascent of Mount Everest written by Sir Edmund Hillary.

5. "Daddy's little girl"

****Dr.Mukta Goyal**

I have this little angel.
For me, she left her wings.
She has no idea how much happiness she truly brings. S
he brightens up my days with her smiles and her laughs.
She helps me to remember all the blessings that I have.

**Tina M. Marascia*

It was a cold day. Ravi and Divya were on their way back from Goa with their son Vasu, who was seven years old. Divya called her mother that her sister-in-law was in the hospital with her delivery pain. She got so excited and shared this news with her husband, after reaching home, without wasting time, and kept their bags and reached the hospital. While waiting outside the labour room, she sat with her brother as he was nervous and needed support. After a couple of hours, suddenly baby's cry came into everyone's ear, and the passage was now filled with full of joy. After a few minutes, the doctor informed us that it was a baby girl. After approximately nine years, we welcomed the girl into our family of four brothers and sisters. Everyone was so happy and congratulated each other. It was Christmas evening, and the joy doubled with the birth of a beautiful daughter. From there, Divya realised that her husband was also felt completeness somewhere with the birth of baby girl of my brother Prashant. After two days, all family members were so excited and waiting at the door to welcome the baby. She has now become the heart of everyone in no time. As the family of Divya was a joint family, everyone was waiting for their turn to hold the baby and to love her. Kids are fighting for their turn, but as she was very small and infants must rest, Mona, Divya's Bhabhi were sent in the room for rest. Regularly, Ravi used to ask Divya to visit the baby girl. He wanted to hold her, spent time with her, but as soon as he held the girl, she used to cry, and everyone was trying to make her busy with rattles and music or, in many ways, but nothing worked. As time passed, the girl now got her beautiful name as Isha started recognising her fuji, and they became friends, but something was still missing in Ravi's life. He started asking his wife to make another change and have their own daughter, but she was not ready for another child and worried that she couldn't handle the child if they had another boy. But after a year, she agreed to take a chance, the couple made a vow in front of God to fulfill their wish, but they were having problems and tried to consult a family doctor, she suggested them the treatment which was not very easy, but they agreed for the same to fulfill their wish. Now they started the treatment, and Ravi was also very much concerned with Divya's health, so he started taking good care of her. The couple kept visiting Isha, whereas the journey of Divya for these nine months was not very simple, it was quite complex, but Ravi always was there for her and helped her and was taking good care of her. After around four months during her ultrasound, Divya asked her doctor to reveal the gender of the child out of curiosity. Still, the doctor refused as it was against his professional ethics.

On the way home after that, she was worried and asked Ravi, What if it is a boy? She could not make up her mind for raising boys, but Ravi made her understand that it is all destiny and we all can't do anything in that, so we should pray to god and leave the rest up to destiny. Finally, a day came when everyone waited for Divya to be taken to the hospital. After waiting for the whole day, the doctor took her to the labor room. Dr. starts congratulating her in just 15 minutes. Divya asks what happened. The doctor says today I did three deliveries, but everyone wanted a girl, but only one was born to you, and I am very happy for you because your heart's wish has come true. As soon as the family members get this news, everyone becomes happy because after 15 years a girl comes to the house and there is no limit to everyone's happiness. Everyone's whole life was complete, it seemed as if their family was complete, and this little soul fulfilled the incompleteness that was there, and she came to this world as an angel for her father. Girls are the most beautiful gift, more than any gift we have to take care of, and only those who are lucky get this priceless gift.

6. Checkmate

****Dr Jyoti Patil**

Raju is broken and shaken to the hilt. He has never ever thought of it that his life would take such an unexpected turn. Sometimes life plays a game of chess and gives us checkmate at the very critical juncture.

It was a lovely October evening when his father came back home from work, looked a little exhausted and tired with a pale face and crumbled attire. Generally, he used to bring some fruits or eatables as evening snacks, which they all used to relish with a cup of pumping hot tea. But that day he did not bring anything and complained of uneasiness.

CORONA, a deadly viral disease imported from China has started wreaking havoc all over the world since March that year. Newspapers, Television channels, and social media, all were flooded with the news of rapidly spreading COVID19 and the death tolls multiplying with the speed of a supersonic rocket. Ten became hundred and hundred became thousand, and thousand turned into nightmarish numbers counting lacs of people. Scary pictures with hips of dead bodies, and people running helter-skelter on to the streets leaving big cities and trying to go back to their home towns.

It was quite unprecedented to witness and experience such an extraordinary situation. Raju's father started feeling a little giddy, his mother became concerned to see his condition and took his temperature, it was 101 degrees Fahrenheit. It was time to get alarmed and they all got scared to see his condition started deteriorating. Fearing something worst might befall. Their doubts got clear when his pulse rate started going down and his oximeter clicked to a lower denomination. It was confirmed later through the RT-PCR test that Raju's father had contracted COVID 19 and had to be hospitalized quickly.

As he was fighting a tough battle all alone as no one was permitted to stay with him. He was isolated and left all alone in the hands of medical care personnel and to the almighty God. While Raju's mother was waiting at home for her husband to come back home safely, she was home-quarantined herself for others' safety at home, Raju, who had just joined an engineering course, and his little sister, Rakhi who was studying in 8th standard.

Mother had seen his father off at the COVID-test centre. She tested negative while his father was positive with oxygen saturation in the 80s. Little she knew that this was going to be their last moment together. Even then, both were hopeful of their dad's recovery, a sudden oxygen level drop changed their life forever.

His father was kept in the isolation ward with oxygen cylinders for the first two days. He was restless and complained a lot on phone. As per him, the doctors did not even come inside the ward and the oxygen tank went empty in the middle of the night and he couldn't sleep thereafter. Raju tried to contact the hospital staff but no one responded, after repeated calls someone answered and he tried to explain the situation and he assured him that he would do his best.

The same story was repeated the next night, and in desperation, Raju tried to contact some of his medical friends to make sure his father was well attended to which was the only silver lining in the whole experience.

However, his father started showing signs of deterioration and oxygen started dipping further. Somehow, a bed was reported available in the ICU with ventilator support as the patient admitted there was expired last night. It turned out to be a Circle of death.

ICU intensive care unit was another nightmare for them as no doctor or sister bothered to venture near him. Raju had to change the diapers of his father. There was no washroom for patients and he was expected to change the diaper after every discharge. His father used to clang his metallic ring on the handrail of his bed to call him who would rush in after wearing a PPE suit to change the diaper. Spending 18 hours a day in the COVID ward in PPE suits because nurses didn't bother to look inside was quite demoralising. The doctors stayed in their chambers playing mobile games while the ventilators beeped crazily. Raju thought should we call them CORONA warriors or honour them for their exemplary services. Those beeps were the scariest sounds that Raju had ever experienced. He managed to get the Remdesivir and Hexa shots from the black market (for Rs.25000 each) just to make sure he got the best medicines so that his father would get well soon.

The next morning at around 4:45 his oxygen tanked to 30s without any warning right in front of Raju's eyes. He rushed inside the ICU wearing PPE, he screamed for the attending doctor who tried to resuscitate him but nothing worked. Though there was a minor oxygen supply glitch and he held his hand through that period, the last time he touched him, through PPE of course. His mother hadn't slept at all since the last 7 nights, calling every 15 minutes- sobbing, hoping for any good news. And, when it finally happened, Raju could not gather the courage to break the news to her. A pandit ji was chanting Mahamrityunjay Mantra for his father at home, while mother was reciting Gayatri Mantra frantically with Durga Saptashati over and over again.

When Raju called his mother to break this heartbroken news that his father was no more, she refused to believe it, instead of asking to take good care of his father. Another blow was in waiting when the hospital authority refused to hand over his dead body as per the CORONA protocol fearing the viral infection. Raju was sent back all alone only after a huge medical bill was paid.

Mother was completely shattered and stunned to find herself in the whirlpool of the unfathomed vacuum of losing him forever. Raju was her only solace and hope to drag on with life. Despondent Raju has lost the game with death. In the game of chess, this was the ultimate checkmate for him with no option of survival.

7. Rumman

****Mamta**

"In life nothing exists in isolation, either in our physical state or in our psyche, we always observe ourselves in different types of combos." Says Mrs. Malti in her last speech to her students at her retirement party. Mrs. Malti, a headmistress of the school, after remembering her carrier of almost thirty-two years, was water-eyed. She consoles herself, as she usually does, and continues, "As we know the combos are in vogue these days, so as our emotions are always in a hybrid state. When we come into this world, the child cries and the mother smiles, at marriage time the bride experiences two types of emotions, as she is going to be separated from her parents and the entire household, and simultaneously, she carries with her the dreams for her new family and new household. Today, I am also sailing in a boat in the sea of an amalgam of emotions."

Mrs. Malti is not a woman of a few words, in fact, she is a complete book. Every chapter begins with a different segment. Her life has been an adventure, as a girl child she had a step-mother, not in the real sense of the word, but her mother wanted a boy, so with her birth, Malti had left her mother a few steps behind, and she was not able to get the true love and care of a real mother. She had a passion for study, her mother directed her towards house-making, but she put her efforts to cultivate her passion while performing her household duties. Even, married life was not as satisfactory as she or every girl dreamed. Her husband was already in a relationship that was not materialized, she became his life partner but could find a place in his heart. He was an army man, lost her life in the early years of life and Malti got a school teacher job as compensation. There begins a new chapter in her life, she embarked on a journey full of happiness and satisfaction. She had no issue but treated all her students like her own kids. And the students also treated her as a mother and shared with her so many talks from their personal life. Malti found a combo of emotions as she lost her husband and got a job where she met with little pure-hearted companions with whom she developed an affectionate relationship.

Rumman was her student like others but with a difference. Rumman called her Malti mam, and beard a special bond with her. Rumman had no mother and was brought up by a father only. Her father was a farmer and Rumman used to give some vegetables and sometimes milk to Malti who lived in the neighborhood. Rumman used to spend more time with Malti during childhood, but now she is married and lives in a nearby village. There was a time when Rumman fell sick and Malti took care of her like a mother. Once, Malti met an accident, and Rumman was coming back from her college. She immediately took her to the hospital and gave blood to Malti helped in saving her life.

The speech continues, "Dear students you think that I am your teacher, but in some ways, you are my teacher. When I failed to solve the difficult problems of life, you tiny, lovely saints taught me to give them another chance. You are so pure-hearted souls, that if you fight for something, you resolve the matter next moment. Two of them have some issues and are not ready to even hand-shake, the surprising thing is that I see you both sharing the meal the very next day. We, so-called mature human beings, burn ourselves in the hurting waves even after years."

Rumman became a nurse in a hospital, and was always ready to leave no stone unturned to help her patients. And also get the same affection from them. Whenever she came to the village, she never forgot to meet Malti who has become a white-haired gesture now. As the retiring month was coming, Malti invited Rumman to her retirement party in advance. Rumman was also excited to go there. She also shared the talk with her cocliques. All the arrangements were done by the school officials. Malti sent messages to her favorite students. As it was the only occasion of celebration for her, she wanted to share this moment of her life with all the people close to her heart. Apparently, we observe hardly any bitter moment in her professional life. She used to share good repo with almost all her cocliques, but sometimes Mr. Jugnu, a clerk in the office tried to resist her file. She communicated with the principal, explained her part, and the clerk had to bow down.

"……*literally I have no kids of my own, but God has gifted me so many children. I treat them like my own, and they also give me the same love. I think like nature, life also completes itself, these tiny tots have filled all corners of my life with love and affection. At this moment of life, I am feeling satisfied. No wishes, no regrets, no expectations either…..*"

"*Dear ones, life is all about balance, the balance between expectation and acceptance, the balance between giving and take, between body and soul, between personal, social, and professional life. My children, life is full of opportunities, only the sky is the limit, believe in your dreams, and make a plan of execution, be focused, and go ahead.*"

Rumman was all set to attend the farewell party, as she was to leave an emergency case arrived and she got busy. She was doing her duty and the mind was occupied with the memories of Madam Malti. Rumman was thinking how Malti used to motivate her at every step of life, she taught her how to decide the priorities in life and to concentrate on them. She wanted to attend the party in any situation but predicted little hope now. She was missing Malti like her mother, she had some plans in her mind about how she would spend time with Malti after retirement. She wanted to go first to the temple on nearby hills, then to Kashmir, then Mount Abu in Rajasthan and the list went long.

"*Go ahead…*" *the students were listening attentively…. "But this going is not easy, as the way of life is not a smooth ride. Sometimes it is a roller coaster, time flows like wind, but there are some days which you will find difficult to pass. The journey of life also has some unexpected obstacles difficult to cross. My dear lovely kids, you no need to be afraid, believe in yourselves, and 'miles to go'. Two more important things you have to keep in mind, are the issues you should focus on, and the issues you should not focus on. You are the writer of the script of your life, you are the editors of your daily routine. It is completely upon you, that where you are going to invest your time and energy. There are some black holes, the type of people, who try to consume your power, and you feel drift from your goal. Be focused, and let anyone sit on the driver seat of your life."*

Rumman was sad now, she wanted to be with Malti on her auspicious day. She was trying her best. One more incident was recurring in her mind, it was the time when she had just started school. Her father was not educated, so he insisted her study with the neighborhood girls, but she was not convinced, and wanted to be taught by her father only. Her father tried his best, but the situation remained the same. Then at last, Mrs. Malti came into the scene and started to teach Rumman daily. And with Malti, Rumman came into the wonderful world of education. They began to spend evenings together. Rumman also recalled their visit to a village fair on Baisakhi. They spend the evenings together; all the moments were clicking in Rumman's mind while doing her duties.

Malti is feeling emotional, her eyes sometimes become watery,.....and then she tries to balance herself with the current situation. Her eyes now are looking for Rumman, but not able to trace..... "You, my dear children... are my companions in life, I have spent all dark movements with you, celebrated every festival with you, …you are part and parcel of my life." Malti feels uneasy,…begins to take breath with difficulty….She tries to step down from the stage….but she falls down. As she falls… she falls in Rumman's arm, who has reached with her husband there after completing her duty. Both read each other's eyes…which were full of tears. Malti could not speak a single word…her pulse was slowing down… Rumman sensed the situation, and she began to cry…"no…no….it can't be happened…..no…Amma….no….You can't leave me alone….no….no……." And now Malti was no more…she left everyone with eyes full of tears…

Rumman was weeping and her husband was trying to console her…The next morning Rumman was sitting with her father….looking towards a new beginning…with so many lessons learnt from Mrs. Malti. The bond was very strong, and it will remain forever…..till her last breath.

8. Munuswamy

****B. V.Siva Prasad**

"Munuswamy, is it fair on your part? We have been together for the past 40 years. But you kept silent and non-reactive when I was being mercilessly slain. Why the hell did you want to finish me?"

"Please do not mistake me. There was no other option left. That's why I kept quiet when they were murdering you," Munuswamy.

"Did you not think of the attachment we have with each other?"

"Please forgive me, mother. I struggled a lot mentally, and it was quite an ordeal for me to accept the proposal, but there was no other choice," Munuswamy apologized in a weepy tone and tears were rolling down his cheeks. He felt guilty. He slowly collected himself and said.

"Mother! The crime that we committed is heinous. No doubts about that. But what is to be done now? Please guide me," Munuswamy pleaded.

Munuswamy woke up at once and realized that the conversation he had so far was in a dream. He got up slowly from his bed. It was still dark out there. He heard a few dogs barking at some distance. Munuswamy felt very thirsty and drank a few glasses of water. He could not sleep any further.

**The previous evening, Munusvamy came back home after working in his field (agricultural) from dusk to dawn. His wife Rangamma made hot water ready for him. He bathed and had his dinner. As he was tired, his body surrendered itself to sleep, but his mind was awake and he had a dream. In his dream, mother tree questioned him and took him to the task. It was customary for the farmers of his village to get together under the big old Banyan tree during their leisure time in the evening and chat. Now the tree was felled by the authorities in order to facilitate a road in the village. Munusvamy and other farmers could not object, as there was no other option left. They badly needed a road and in the process had to sacrifice the tree, which was giving them shade and shelter for a long time. But Munusvamy felt very uneasy after the removal of the tree since it was also a home for so many birds like crows, cuckoos, parrots, and others. The farmers and villagers used to rest under the tree and they revered it like they respect their mother. Munuswamy became quite emotional after they ground the tree and his late mother, Narayanamma's thoughts, occupied his mind.*

**Munuswamy was born and brought up in a small village known as Muthukur. His father Venkayya died while working on his farm when the lightning struck. Munuswamy was a kid. As he grew older and was gaining the power of discrimination, he was told by the residents of his village,*

"Your father was a gentleman and also a Good Samaritan (a man possessing helping nature). He was very kind-hearted and

was maintaining a good rapport with other farmers like us in the village. He was not chasing money and used to help others who were in need"

After the untimely and unexpected death of her husband, Narayanamma went through a lot of hardships and raised Munusvamy. She cultivated her own piece of land and earned a livelihood. She also could send Munusvamy to a school that was in the neighboring village. Narayanamma was even prepared to send him for higher studies by raising a loan. But Munusvamy was not willing, and he started working with his mother in cultivation.

He had a passion for farming by participating in the activities like plowing, seeding, watering, cutting crops, and other related activities. He just was passionate and abundantly in love with the land. Plants and trees were very dear to him. He used to feel a lot whenever he heard about the felling of trees and tried his best to stop such activities. His mother, Narayanamma was also loved plants and greenery. She passed away 5 years ago.

Felling off the Banyan tree in his village disturbed Munuswamy a lot. He turned moody and remained aloof from others for a few days. He kept his distance even from his wife, Rangamma. Munuswamy often was seeing the poor tree appearing in his dreams. One day, while he was working in his field, an idea and suggestion offered by the tree (in his dreams) flashed through his mind. He wanted to implement it.

*So far, Munuswamy was using fertilizers abundantly. As a result, he ended up having enormous debts. Drought conditions *were prevailing, and he had to pay high-interest amounts on the loans he had raised. As a result, he had to sell some portion of his land. One day in a program on TeleVision, they explained how trees and plants would be helpful in improving the economic condition of the farmers. This inspired and motivated him to think of plantations. He started off by planting around 100 Teak plants in his land. Within a year, he expanded his activity by planting different plants like mango, cashew, tamarind, red sandal, amla, and others.*

Within 5 years, his field started looking like a forest. Now he owned 14 acres of land in which several varieties of trees were growing. There was a significant change in his attitude. Earlier, he used to be temperamental. Rangamma one day observed,

"There is a sea of change in you now. You used to get annoyed and shout at me frequently. Now you are a different person and seem to be thrilled with yourself. What's the reason?"

"Yes, Ranga! Growing these plants is giving me immense happiness. The cows and buffalos have become dearer to me. I feel that if our son is interested; let's make him study a course in agriculture and improve his skills in improving our cultivation. A lot of students nowadays are after software jobs. Either they prefer to work in big cities or migrate to foreign countries., they are neglecting our villages. If everyone follows the same path, then what is the fate of agriculture in our country?" Munuswamy lamented.

Rangamma found the reason for what her husband was saying. She added,

"Yes, you're right. We follow our culture and tradition here. I don't think that the people living in towns care about these things. In fact, I would love to live and die in our village"

Now their son Srinivasulu and daughter Manga help their parents with the cultivation. Plants and livestock became a top priority for Munusvamy. Even though they cannot converse with him, he can connect and communicate with them through their body language. One day the black cow, a favorite of Munusvamy, fell ill. He could read its pain through its eyes and immediately took it to the veterinary hospital and got it treated. Another time, the Jasmine creepers appeared dull. He did the needful. He started empathizing with the plants and the animals raised by him on his farm. Now he owned the pains of his plants and animals alike. He can understand now the relation existing among various species of living and non-living things existing on the earth. In a better manner. He became more energetic and enthusiastic about life.

Mr Purushottam, the Agricultural Officer told Munuswamy one day

"Munuswamy, even the earth has life. We should not pollute it with fertilizers and insecticides which contain harmful chemicals. Please use only the organic methods for your cultivation"

He also imparted training. One day Munuswamy asked Mr Purushottam,

"Sir, my son Srinivasulu wants to pursue a course on agriculture. How to go about it?"

"Munusamy! Since your son has got good academic credentials and has got an aptitude for agriculture. Please join him in B. Sc (Agriculture) course. He can even study further if he is interested," Purushottam said and guided them through the entire process.

*A few years passed by. One morning the telephone rang at Munuswamy's house.

"Hello! Tree Munuswamy here. May I know who is speaking?" Munuswamy said,

"Hi, I am Thirupataiah and am calling from a village called Phirangipuram, which is pretty close to you," the gentleman replied

"We are going to conduct a health awareness program for the elderly and senior citizens next Sunday and I extend my invitation to you to be the chief guest on the occasion," Thirupataiah added.

"Certainly, but please make sure you plant some saplings on the occasion, at selected locations in your village," Munuswamy said.

"As you wish, Mr Munuswamy! We all are pretty aware that you wouldn't attend any program where the planting of saplings is not a part" Thirupataiah. Munuswamy kept himself busy in helping his fellow farmers in their cultivation of land and raising plants by providing suitable suggestions. His son, Mr. Srinivasulu completed his research studies in agriculture and is working as a scientist. Whereas his son-in-law(his daughter Ms. Manga's husband runs a nursery in a neighboring village.

*One fine morning, Munuswamy told his wife

"I had a wonderful dream last night, Ranga. My mother appeared in it as a tree and she said, 'My son, please make sure you make people plant a lot of saplings in and around and play your role in increasing the green belt. The more the greenery, the happier and merrier we are!'"

Rangamma smiled in acknowledgment. The trees and plants in their backyard moved their branches and leaves in agreement. The cattle and calves also nodded by swaying their heads.

****(Dedicated in love to Mr. Maram Thangasamy of Tamil Nadu)***

9. Children Of India's Defence

**S.Nithianandham

Jaihind is the manthra

Which run in their blood

The courage which sparks

And glowing their eyes

The Cardinals of discipline

Which is their soul

The josh like fire which projects

The dedication towards

Their actual heart India proud

Peninsular nation and he

The son of Indian defence

Like land air and sea

And the Indian defence son the NCC

10. "The Golden Feast"

**S.Nithianandham

Move on to kiss?the mount with shy,
He asks the air? to join with them,
The peak, he extended as a,
An enormous range of hills,??OH WOW!
There's a nice fragrance of flowers,
They call the butterflies ?from,
The miles of hills to dwell with Joy fills,
The mount has many bogs, surrounded
With some fog, there scenes more
It's High from the seashore...,
The creek from the brook,
It is crook and crook, Aye see!
There are some dots with the horns
Deer ? and doe with dotted fur,
They hath an eminent hair,
Crooking Brooks calls thine,
To taste the grasses fine,
Deer sends a signals there,
Through sounds of cuckoos fair,

Cuckoo send a beauty wish,
To swimming joyous Golden fish ?,
It tells the brook very calm,
That his friends reach the fairest farm,
He welcomes thine by making them shine,
He has told some fun that he is a gift of sun,
They want first to take rest,
Cloths of Arras is the best,
He asked them for dinner,
The tasty sweets are very thinner,
Make the feast more delight,
With the beauty of sunlight,
All the animals come there,
To saw the eminent hair,?
Eyes ? of flowers open slow,
With the help of sunny ☀? glow,
Deer and doe want to move to,
Brook and trees?? thanking too,
The farewell feast was taking by,
Lovely words of bye..bye..bye...!

11. "Surpassing Horizons: Salute to Bhawana Kanth"

** *Dr. Rachna Rastogi*

Culminating the National fervour
Came the debut of The Dassault Rafale.
Fortifying chivalry of Tri-colour
Resounded "burst of fire"
French twin-engine hinged with canard delta wing,
Multirole fighter aircraft, gorged its golden ring.
Rafale, literally meaning "Guest of Wind",
Can board the skies;
With the speed of wind,
The splendour it magnifies,
With gust perfectly aligned.
Rarest moment of pride and glory,
Brought the nation a gallant story.
Breathe holding, spectacular spectrum,
As if Sun rays passing through electrum.
Brimming hearts filled with joy,
Lieutenant Bhawana Kanth flew the plain like a toy,

And left the foe in despair,
When flew the Raffle to the air.
Showed the world her unflinching flair.
History created and reaffirmed the faith,
That a woman can be the saviour.
None the less woman can be a fighter, protector, and creator.
Salute to the indomitable spirit of a fighter,
Enchantingly captivating Rafale shining brighter.

12. La...La...La...Laa...

**S.Nithianandham

La...la...la..
Run OH a baby runs,
And needs a happy fun,
Lot's of stars there
Which sparks like
A beauty fair, OH!
Here my dear moon
It's like the head of
My silver spoon
My mom starts to sing
La..la ...la...la
Sweet sleep my vennila
I have now swept
In a dream ocean.

13. The Epitome Of Rain

**Prerna Sharma

Let me be mad
In the madness of soul,
No blaze in the
Gloom of mortal coal.
Let me shine
In the solace of mine,
In a world of illusions
They confine.
Let me revive the self
In a journey of lamented land,
Songs of love
Sing the gritty sand.
Let me learn
From the finest of all,
The art that
Nobody ever told,
Shall rise and born
In the heart and soul
A treasure of memories to recall,

There comes the redemption of all.

14. The Insatiable Curiosity

** *Prerna Sharma*

Who will pacify my quest?
The souls bedizened with a perishable blanket,
Who will foster my quest?
The bards dancing beneath the broken casket,
Will they emerge again and again?
To shine on the indigent world in pain,
We search all but all in vain.
My question flows to them again,
Who will write my quest?
The ones penning the bogus crafts of living,
Burning ink on the paper,
Tells the drifting saga of our creator,
I wonder what would be the shade of truth,
Shall be seen with dwindling youth,
Still my quest shan't cease and appease.
Who will come for my quest?
Without you, I won't take any rest.
I hope you shan't come,
As the quest is mine,

Shall be forgotten another time,
Like a drop, buried and oblivious in the aisles,
Aware is the ocean that has travelled the miles.

15. COVID'19

Ms. Bhuvaneswari Srikanthan

Shut down
Curtains shut down
Transport shut down
Schools shut down
Industries shut down
Worldwide all human activities
Of in and out officially shut down
That couldn't shut down
This can reach and suck human soul...
It sucked lakhs
World struck
Couldn't struggle with it...
No burden borders
No religious relishes
World struck
Couldn't struggle with it
It sucked lakhs
Finally 'IT' can controlled
But IT'S another version started..

World ready to struggle
World struck.
Curtain down again!

16. The Lord

Dr. Saroj Bala

O Lord of the people/Ganas
The auspicious one
May your guidance
Enlighten my path.
The world is full of
Bhasmasur and Tarakasur
May your gift of wisdom
Illuminate dark recesses of mind.
Carnal pleasure rules
The human realm
May your supreme aura
Fill my existence with piety.
O brother of Murugan
Whose world is his parents' feet
Lead me to the godhead within
Dispelling the arresting fear
The most precious one
The remover of obstacles
Bestow strength to this corporeal vessel

To vanquish evil within and without

17. Thanksgiving

****Dr.Saroj Bala**

O ethereal Mother
Your grace sanctifies souls
Your endless bounty
Fills our coffers aplenty
O the celestial and imperishable one
Your magnanimous mien
Grants immeasurable largesse
Sparkling divinity of your presence
Quells all corporeal impulses
And Power of your boons
Turns misery into beatitude
Accept our thanksgiving
For the benediction
Our obeisance to you for
The sacralised life itself

18. Soul's cry

****Ms. Bhuvaneswari Srikanthan**

Summer vacation!
Before COVID '19
Visit to Native
Rest from academic
Entertainment and Enjoyment
Summer Courses
Extra curricula
After COVID
Lockdown
Online classes
Part time jobs
Economic poverty
Deaths
Mutation
Vaccination
Breaking News
Political changes
Expectations
Third waves

Precautions
Prevention
Medicines
Mutation in lifestyle
Hand wash, masks and gloves,
Stream inhalation
Herbal juice
Returned to old games
Food habit
New Life style
Hope to overcome COVID
And save future generations!

19. Rocks

Ms. Bhuvaneswari Srikanthan

Rocks can speak and smile,
It depicts the Puranas and society,
It represents the culture and wisdom,
It kindles our soul to know our ancestors amazing talent,
It throws many scientific facts,
It depicts various art and culture,
It creates curiosity to know astronomy,
It is great credit to the society,
But it won't reveals its sculptor,
But throughout the ages it attracts the human,
And makes him to bow and do Research forever,
IT is the Indian sculpture!

20. Ignite Oneself

****Dr. Capt. Indrani M R**

Thoughts are Tossing and travelling
Within and struck my mind,
Drive oneself to do what you dream,
Mind and heart doesn't listen to me
But say the inner voice to be strong forever.
The wounded soul is blessed and bestowed
With the memories of loved ones,
But the darkness of my past,
Have the trace within, which never fades.
The buried sorrows convey words with fear and anger.
Pertinent questions rise within
Can I run away from my responsibilities?
Can I run away from my destiny? No I Can't!
Then, where shall I run knowing the truth?
Life has sulk to the blues!
The Moon and the Sun teach
Us to lit the future with light,
The prettiest eyes have cried the most tears,
And the kindest heart has felt the most pain

Amidst this I must prevail with perfection!
Learn to live with challenges,
Learn to live with uncertainty of life,
Learn to fight against the struggle to meet the ends,
And leave the legacy behind,
From untraded path to trodden.
Burn those traits of nasty and arrogance,
Ignite to live upright with morality,
Promise oneself to live
Harmonious development of positivity,
And cherish the best traits of life and create a world
Where love and respect be eternal.

21. In The Journey Of Life Being A Tractor

**V Taruna*

In the journey of Life being a tractor
Trying to prove myself of being a benefactor,
What if the world measures my skills using a protractor?
Will I be able to save them through my factor?
The life with no laughter
Seems to be a slaughter,
Never mind, Never mind of being a raptor
But my pure heart is like a nectar.
Oh my Dear, Why do you fear?
The sunny days where the clouds are clear,
Make the heart start with a cheer
Set way until the earth is your peer.

22. As Long as a Lake

V. Taruna

As long as a lake
When do we get a chance to take?
We need to wait for other's sake
To show them how we make.
We work throughout the week
But what do we seek?
Try to be mild and meek
To show them how you freak
Life is as enjoyable as we are
But we need to go far,
To do good things that fills the jar
Try to be spotless without a scar.

23. January January…

V. Taruna

January, January where have you been?
February, February have you seen?
March , March are you a teen?
April , April you are the Queen.
May ,May Is it your day?
June ,June make your way,
July ,July shine like a ray
August, August What do you say?
September, September jump like a frog
October, October chill in the fog,
November, November enjoy your jog
December ,December where is your dog?

24. Everywhere Everywhere…

****V. Taruna**

Everywhere Everywhere we have buildings
But I have my siblings,
Who are as sweet as a cherry
And I hope they are merry.
Everywhere Everywhere we have roads
But we hurry in our loads,
Let's take some rest
To do our best.
Everywhere Everywhere we have trees
Which give us air as fast as deers,
Life does not matter on income
It depends on how we welcome.

25. It Is An Ancient Place…

**V. Taruna

It is an ancient place of the era
Filled with glamour and aura,
Richness of oils such as lavender
Time passes as we turn the pages of the calendar.
It is our beloved Country India
People with joy playing Dandiya,
By singing the classical music
Making it much more cosmic.
Cultural Heritage is the country's leisure
There are many, we cannot measure,
Tourists come here to take pleasure
That's the reason, Why it is treasure.

26. It Is The Time...

****V.Taruna**

It is the time to stay at home
Where we are forbidden to roam,
Getting back to the tradition
To survive and protect our generation.
In this situation of pandemic
People struggle to end this epidemic,
To save lives of living
By giving.
Arise , Arise to spread the word
So that it is heard,
Let us be brave and competent
To show the world that we are confident.

27. Just Like The Waters...

**V. Taruna

Just like the waters flow
We pray and bow
To attain peace and glow
And learn lessons from a crow.
In this scorching heat
Girls oil their hair and pleat,
People struggling in the metro to get a seat
Musicians discover a new beat.
Life is as different as everyone thinks
Prayer and patience is what it links,
But anger and darkness shrinks
Yet we must open our eyes that blink.

28. To be a Buddha

Dr. Swarnamayee Purohit

I knew I would never defeat the Sun -
The eternal light
But with the blinks I wanted to show that
I could lead him onto the unknown country
Where millions of stars persuade me to fight
I solved the puzzle
Unscrambled the mystery
I knew I couldn't annihilate the unwanted impulses
But I could have trampled the thorny weeds
That injured my feelings
Each drop of my blood that the earth succumbed
Could be digested by the worms
I loved to climb the stairways
That could help me avenge my dwarfness
Against the Almighty
My hunger my thirst
That couldn't be satiated
I knew
To be a Buddha

Needed to be jatismaras
To be incarnated as bodhisatwas
I sat beneath the Bodhi tree
Controlled my senses
But my appetite still prevalent
Hindered my journey
I lost my shadow
And clung to the ultimate soul:
That's my goal.

29. Reborn out of Fire

Dr. Swarnamayee Purohit

That day
She lost her childhood
When she became the second mother of her little brother
She missed plucking berries
Smelling the fragrance of the papers of her books
Listening tales about Draupadi being borne out of fire
Astonished to know Sita being rescued unburnt from fire.
That day she lost her adolescence
When she was sent with
Nay sold to the Contractor
Her new lovely dress
Enchanting but throwing her into the gutter.
That day she thought
She was redeemed
When exchanged garlands with the young engineer.
That day she lost her motherhood
When He took her to the doctor
When her womb was auctioned- a surrogate mother she became.
That day she lost herself

When the baby she delivered was thrown into the bin
She rushed and hold her fragile body
In her arms
The baby-
She was fire
She was Sita
She was Draupadi
Reborn out of the fire
Out of her womb — the altar of fire.

30. The Prince of a mother's tale

****Dr. Swarnamayee Purohit**

A child lost his parents
But proclaims he is not an orphan
In the morning
The breeze wakes him up
Like his mother kisses his forehead
Touches his cheeks.
The Sun pours his heart
With brightness of optimism
Like his father who consoles him
With chocolates and cookies.
At night when opens his window
The moon soothes his heart
With such a somber glance.
The stars together
Stimulate his feelings
They put his little ailing body into the shroud of darkness.
He dreams

His mother holding him on her arms
His father holding him on his shoulder
And he is picking flowers
The trees are bending their boughs
And he is being touched by something mesmerizing.
How can the invisible virus
Make him orphan
The child knows
He will fight and kill
The invisible demon
Yes, he is the Prince of his mother's tale
And will save the whole humanity.

31. Ashes

Disha Madan

Ruffle-less life
Calm waves of life
Inevitable silence
Subtle voices
All muster in to a peaceful ocean.
An ocean of peace,
Peeps in to the life of spirituals,
Seeps there where fertility of mind resides,
Running in to the hides and corners
Of the Soul sublime.
Oh ! If only I could beget it,
I would nurse it unto eternity,
Lying close to it,
I would never depart it,
Weaving it in to my heart, mind and body.
Life's forsaken,
Life-heart beats hurt,
Each breath sounds sulking
Corners of mind ooze out to unconsciousness,

Lacerated heart, mind, body wriggle thro' existence
Aloof, far away from the peaceful ocean,
Searching far and wide,
'But unable to spot,
A wave of peace – tis next to impossible,
Boiling in to the cauldron of pangs of torture.
Oh! If I could beget
A piece of peace – ocean,
Burning in fire,
Where is peaceful ocean,
The extremes of heat
Flames twist the mind – heart in to a heap of Ashes.

32. A Signature of Life

**** *Disha Madan***

A signature of life,
Rushes boundlessly,
Procuring an illusion,
Illuminating misconceptions,
Delivering routes of incessant fire.
Drawing life with varied colors,
Reflecting its own image;
Heat, rain, cold join in,
With an air of discontent,
Blossoming in the region of heartlessness.
Borrowed breaths,
Circulating in this universe,
Sharing reverses and ruins,
With the enchanting physiques,
Of dead stock.
Behold! Pull in and watch,
You and me in the signature of life.

33. Aromatic Fragrance

**Dr. Susheela. B

It's been a long time
Walking into a Coffee Shop
Longing for a cup of Coffee
With an ambiguous smile!
A warm and cozy corner
With lots of mixed emotions
Nobody but You and Me
Surrounded by glacing fence
Undoubtedly farthest from my mind, hence…
Aromatic Coffee with dark brown shade
And dream steam
Lovely fragrance, dressed in milky cream
Urge to have it with gorgeous and
Nostalgic sentiments
To beat the heap of forlorn thoughts
That are not to be felt!
Ah! Coffee at Night
Makes me awake!!

34. Rock n Roll

Disha Madan

Rolling on the rocking earth,
Rummaging even the terminating,
Groping for the unknown object,
Looking gay but fretful inside,
This is a man in the bosom of the earth.
Peep into the past,
A reflection of the self,
Marks in the subconscious,
A home of confusions and dilemmas,
To be that or this !!!
Forgetful of the ocean of love,
From where we enlighten;
Surrounded by if's and buts;
Making the self a complicated affair,
Putting to task the innocent heart,
Am I awake or in slumber?
Is this the chart of life,
Or the memory account?
Of whilst I pay the debts due,

DR. ALOK DR. MUKTA

Surfacing the imbalance of the events innumerable,
Can one ever clear the floating debt ???
Embarking on the science of pleasure,
Can I spot a word of peace?
Whispering into the veins of strain,
I pause to breathe into the crevice,
To register me in the annals of,
The Fortune – Writer,
Who is
The Reservoir of all goodness and of all joys.

35. Subtle World

D. Sasi Devi

Signing off the sound world
Shiva ushered to the subtle movie world
Snow white squashy world
Sedate movements in the shining world
Scintillating subtle beings
Selfless souls, springs of solace
Saturated in the strength of the soul
Swinging and singing in silence
Shimmering rays of silver spread
Spiritual silence reigns and signs
Subtle world – silent saccharine sojourn
Sojourn heading to the sovereign.

36. I

****D. Sasi Devi**

I swim like a fish, in the ocean of love
I dive deep, discover the divine pearl
I wait to hold, the holy hand
I love to walk, holding hands, into heaven
I bask in the Supreme soul
I bloom in the divine warmth
I remain silent and simple
I churn the divine knowledge
I remember the inheritance
I am surpassed by the bliss.

37. Soul Shines

D. Sasi Devi

Soul shines, the body vanishes
Virtues bloom, vices fade
Bliss pervades, misery recedes
Silence speaks, noise silences
Selflessness rises, selfishness buries
Soul radiates, darkness disappears
Love embraces, hatred excludes
Essence energizes, elaborateness discharges
Celibacy empowers, lust sins
Brotherhood unites, enmity divides.

Author's Bio

Dr. Koganti Vijay Babu

Dr. Koganti Vijay Babu is popularly known as Vijay Koganti and is a Professor of English. He is now working as Academic Officer monitoring assessment and accreditation aspects of the Govt. degree colleges under the commissionerate of collligeate education of Andhra Pradesh.

Dr. Alok Chandra

Dr. Alok Chandra is currently working as an Assistant Professor in the Department of English at Sri Abiraami Arts and Science College for Women, Gudiyattam, Vellore, Tamilnadu.He is a poet, critic, reviewer, and editor who hails from Bargaon, Nalanda,BIhar. He has been rendering his active editorial services as the co-editor of The Creative Launcer:An International Journal of English. He is the former research scholar of Nava Nalanda Mahavibara(Deemed to be University), under ministry of culture, Govt. of India, Nalanda, Bihar. He has participated and presented his research papers in National and International conferences/ seminars and also attended relevant workshops on ELT. He has got his well researched papers in published in international journals and edited books.He always displays his hearty passion for composing his poems concerning the global ecology: his poems have been published in both journals and anthologies, He is the recipient of best research paper award in a national conference for his paper entitled'The poetry of Gray Synder:An Echology Perspective'.organized by the Dept. of English, Andhra Loyola Institute of Engineering and Technology, Vijaywada, Andhra Pradesh.

Dr Joseph Kumar Kakumanu

Dr Joseph Kumar Kakumanu is a 2021 PhD in English literature awarded from Andhra University. He has 25 years of teaching experience. He started his career in Chandrapur, MS as a teacher soon after his B.Ed. in 1993 and promoted to a Junior Lecturer and then back in A.P he worked as Asst. Professor, English. Currently, he is working as a Professor at Loyola Institute of Technology and Management, Guntur, Andhra Pradesh. He is also a freelance writer and writes content for websites. Besides, he takes flair in writing poems, songs. He writes songs in Telugu, English and Shayari in Hindi. He even composes music and orchestrates the same with his voice. He takes interest in event management in the college. Scripts for all the cultural events. Trains the students in communication skills in connection with the campus placements. Having been a creative writer, he prefers writing thematically. He has got his poems and papers published in Journals and edited books. He also leads the Church Choir. Currently, he is working on releasing his own book of Poems and a Devotional Album.

Dr. Deepesh Kr. Thakur

Dr. Deepesh Kr. Thakur, faculty of English in DIT University, Dehradun, having PhD., MA in English -Linguistics, MBA(Finance) & DCA from BRA Bihar University, Muzaffarpur (Bihar), native of a village-Kansi, Darbhanga (Bihar), having thirteen years of rich experience in teaching-supervising the Ph.D., PG & UG students in University & corporate sector, NSN Ltd. India, Visiting Faculty in LIMT, Faridabad, administrative position held in World College of Technology & Management (WCTM), Gurgaon, as a Coordinator of Applied Science, Book Authored, 'English Language for Professional & Technical Education', Germany, books of B.Ed. & M.Ed., presented forty research papers presented-published in International & National Conference proceedings, published a dozen of papers in reputed Journals & Twelve chapters' in edited books. Editing International Journal, 'Mirrorview' (USA-Germany) & IJER (India) & Magazine-WCTM Pulse, research interests in English Language Teaching, English Literature, Linguistics, Translation Studies, Indian English Writing, Diasporic Literature, Management, Maithili, Sanskrit, Hindi, Nepali & Bengali.

Dr Mukta Goyal

Dr Mukta Goyal is a dedicated professional having an experience of almost a decade in academia. Presently she is working as a Principal in Manvi Institute of Edu. &Tech, Delhi, SCERT. She has completed her Ph. D. in Management from Mewar University, Chittorgarh. She has been conferred with the "Best Principal "Award in the year 2022 along with "The Real Super Woman" Award in the year 2020. She holds her credit to author four books and also edited around nineteen books with different titles.She is also a regular columnsist in newspapers and very much acclaimed for her poetries.Many of her research papers have been acknowledged and published in the Journal of National and International repute as well as conference proceedings too.

Dr Jyoti Patil

Dr Jyoti Patil *professionally holds an administrative post of a principal in a local college in Nagpur with 33 years of teaching experience. Basically she is poet at heart and a creative writer by passion. Her poems and stories have been published in various magazines, books, journals and national dailies. She has also published an anthology of her poems titled Living beyond Life (2018) composed mostly on nature and life. She has received Golden Book of Records' recognition for her poems on Corona in 2020 appeared in GEM III.*

Mamta

Mamta is an M.A. English, M. Phil. and currently pursuing her Ph.D. from the Research Centre, GCG-11, Panjab University, Chandigarh, India. She has served her duties as an Assit. Prof. at Dyal Singh College, Karnal, D.A.V. College Abohar, Punjab, and S.G.G.S. College sec.-26, Chandigarh. In eight years of experience of teaching English language and literature, she taught both U.G. and P.G. classes. Besides, she has participated and presented research papers at the National and International level seminars and conferences. She has published a book and several research articles in different National and International journals. She has contributed chapters for several Books on different topics. She is a member in the Editorial Board of Edwin Group of Journals. She has participated in various workshops on the topic like, creative writing, translation studies, recent research trends, latest teaching techniques in English, etc. Her carrier objectives are to excel in the field of Education and Research.

B.V.Siva Prasad

Siv(B. V. Siva Prasad) is a short story writer, Poet, Novelist, Translator, and Essayist in both Telugu and English languages. He is the recipient of the prestigious 'Ampasayya Naveen Literary Trust Award' for his Telugu novel entitled 'Harivillu' which got published in 2017.

S.Nithianandham

Department of English and foreign language, BHARATHIAR UNIVERSITY, Coimbatore

S. Nithianandham is pursuing his PG degree in English literature from Bharathiar University, Coimbatore (Tamilnadu)

Dr. Rachna Rastogi

Former Professor, Dean Student Affairs & SM Club Coordinator, at GLA University Mathura & Gsfc University, Vadodara. Dr. Rachna Rastogi is a Freelance Writer, Corporate-Trainer, Poet and Social activist. She had been the Bio-Farma, Elsevier journal reviewer for Language. Dr. Rastogi is a Certified Trainer for Human Values and Professional Ethics form IIT Kanpur did her P.hD. in 2003 from Ruhilkhand University, has attended various short term courses on Soft Skills form IIT Roorkee, & Kanpur and has to her credit various research papers & poems published in journals and chapters in proceedings and books.

Consecutively for the year 2018 and 2019 Dr. Rastogi has been awarded as best faculty coordinator by IIT Mumbai, Powai, during Tech-radiance.

Dr. Rachna Rastogi has delivered various lectures for corporate trainees like GATL, GIPCL, GSFC Ltd. etc. and has organized 6 weeks long substantial and innovative Foundation Course for B.Tech, MBA and BSc students giving exposure of potential life skills programs i.e. Narcotics Prevention, First Aid, Road Safety, Digital interface, Health and Hygiene, Corporate Ethics etc., in association with eminent faculties form IITs and Government organizations at GSFC University. She has also actively organized a substantial Swachhta drive in and around Vadodara in association with VMC, under the guidance of Mr.P K Taneja, IAS (Rets.) (Former Additional Chief Secretary to Govt. of Gujarat. Dr. Rachna Rastogi has also actively carried the interface between Industry and academia to facilitate value teaching and hands on learning experience for Science, Engineering and Management aspirants.

Prerna Sharma

Being an avid and curious learner, Prerna Sharma has various areas of interest. She obtained a Bachelor's Degree in Journalism & Mass Communication from GGSIPU along with BA Hons English from SOL Delhi University. She is a novice writer who likes to write about the cosmic spirituality, divine mother nature and human predicaments related to irreversible death and the beauty of life. In addition to writing, she is interested in music, art, philosophy, psychology and the deep mysteries of world. She is a final year student of MA English and has worked as a primary school teacher. The key to her living is the positivity within her.

Ms. Bhuvaneswari Srikanthan

Ms.. Bhuvaneswari Srikanthan lives in Chennai and has been working as Assistant Professor of English in Dr. MGR Educational and Research Institute, Deemed to be University, Chennai since 2015. Ms Bhuvaneswari has also 18 years of teaching experience in schools before joining this University. Teaching is not only her profession but also her passion As a teacher she is happy to educate many young minds and kindle their knowledge to grow and develop into good citizens.. She has received many awards and certificates for producing 100% results in University Examinations. Recently Ms. Bhuvaneswari stepped into the world of creative writing.. She has to her credit a sizeable number of publications which include two chapter publications and two publications each in National and International conferences and one in UGC CARE Group.

Dr. Saroj Bala

She joined Delhi College of Engineering as an Assistant Professor in 2000. now she is working as Associate Professor in the department of Humanities at Delhi Technological University. She has presented and published more than 30 papers in National and international journals and conferences, She has received followingawards:

1. *Bhagirathi Samman in 2006 at the Triveni Sabhagar, Mandi House, New Delhi, awarded by Bhagirathi Samajik Sanskritik Manch, Delhi.*

2. *Uday Teacher's Award in 2011 at the LTG Auditorium, Mandi House, New Delhi, awarded by Uday Samajik Sanskritik Manch, Delhi*

3. *National Ambedkar Felloship in 2012 at the 28th National Conference of Dalit Writers by Bhartiya Dalit Sahitya Academy, Delhi.*

4. *Pratibha Shree Samman in 2018*

Membership of Professional Bodies:

a. *Asia TEFL (Life membership)*

b. *Association of English Studies in India (Life Membership)*

c. *Heritage Society, Patna (Annual Membership)*

d. *ELTAI (Long term temporary Membership)*

Area of Interest: *ELT, Indian Mythology, Cultural Studies*

She writes poems and stories in English and Hindi

Dr Capt. Indrani

Dr Capt. Indrani M R is an Assistant Professor of English, NCC officer, Nodal officer for UGC sponsored programs, and Soft Skill Trainer from SBRR Mahajana First Grade College, Mysuru, Karnataka.

V Taruna

Venkatesan Sai Taruni is pursuing Bachelor of Arts in Economics, Public Administration and Political Science in St.Francis college For Women , Begumpet, Telangana. She is from Hyderabadand an alma mater of St.Francis College for Girls Secunderabad and St.Ann's High School , Madinaguda. She was a topper of her school and intermediate college. She started writing poems at the age of 17years. Her hobbies are Poetry, Singing and Painting.

Dr. Swarnamayee Purohit

Reader in English, Laxminarayan College, Jharsuguda, Odisha

Dr. Swarnamayee Purohit presently works as a Reader in English in Laxminarayan College, Jharsuguda, Odisha. She has done her Ph. D in the ideological aspects related to English education (studies) in Odisha, her native state. Her specialization is in Comparative literature, Indian writing in English, Feminine Ideology and Folk literature. She translates essays, stories and poems from English to Odia and Hindi and vice versa. She participates in debates, seminars, conferences,etc. She writes research articles on literary topics as well as on social issues. She contributes literary as well as intellectual articles in different journals, books and anthologies.

Disha Madan

Dr Disha Madan is teaching at the Department of Studies in English at Nehru College & PG Centre, Hubli (Karnataka). She is a creative writing specialist, a social activist, and has published books on American Women Writers and Cultural Studies. She publishes a bi-annual research journal "Impression" for budding research scholars. Recently she has published a novella, ' Crossing Over '.

A well known social figure in the twin cities of Hubli-Dharwad, she was the President of Innerwheel Club of Hubli Mid-Town, IIW Dist 317, for the year 2015-16.

Dr. Susheela. B

She is M.A.[Eng.], M.A [His] B.Ed. .M Phil {Eng.) PhD (Eng.) Dip. In French

- *Worked for 8 years as an ICSE & CBSE Teacher both in India & abroad*
- *Was the Principal for ICSE & CBSE & Composite PU College for 10 years*

- *Currently working as an Associate Professor in Jyoti Nivas College Autonomous*
- *She has published about 30 papers in both national & International level.*
- *She has presented about 12 papers in both national & international level.*
- *Was invited as a Resource to give talks to other Colleges.*

Dr. Susheela is currently working as an Associate professor,Department of English in Jyoti Nivas College, Bangalore. She started her career at school level & has a rich experience in both schools and colleges. She worked for 8 years as an ICSE & CBSE both in India & abroad & 10 years as a Principal for Composite College.She is a recipient of several awards as a teacher and as a Principal. .

As a member of several Social Originations like Blind Association of India, Spastic Society of India, Akshara Old Age home, Anti-Human Trafficking club, Green Peace Association, Spit India Movement, Awareness of Anti-Plastic Association, Part of BBMP Association Awareness in ISRO Layout etc., she has done a lot of social services in these areas.

She has been a part of Tribal Youth Association where she studied on tribals and did Research on them. She travelled widely on this to many mountain ranges including Nepal & North East.

She loves travelling and has travelled widely both in India & abroad. She is an avid reader and is passionate about books. She loves cooking and has conducted several cooking classes.She is a double master's degree holder in both English & History, had done M.Phil.

& Ph.D. in English. She is passionate about Languages and can speak several languages. She also has a Diploma in French & currently pursuing German as well in Bangalore Central University.

D. Sasi Devi

D. Sasi Devi, Assistant Professor of English, Thiagarajar College, Madurai, Tamilnadu. She feels proud to reside in Bharath. What cannot be changed has to be accepted. Positive outlook of life and diligent use of time will pave way to success. World transformation is possible only through self transformation.